ENGLISH
for Primary Schools

book 4

W. P. Cleland

illustrated by
Peter Joyce

Nelson

P7855 English for Primary Schools Bk 4
8/9 Un. 689/696 20 em PAB2

Thomas Nelson and Sons Ltd
Nelson House Mayfield Road
Walton-on-Thames Surrey KT12 5PL
P.O. Box 18123 Nairobi Kenya

116-D JTC Factory Building
Lorong 3 Geylang Square Singapore 1438

Thomas Nelson Australia Pty Ltd
19–39 Jeffcott Street West Melbourne Victoria 3003

Nelson Canada Ltd
81 Curlew Drive Don Mills Ontario M3A 2R1

Thomas Nelson (Hong Kong) Ltd
Watson Estate Block A 13 Floor
Watson Road Causeway Bay Hong Kong

Thomas Nelson (Nigeria) Ltd
8 Ilupeju Bypass PMB 21303 Ikeja Lagos

Revised edition 1976
Reprinted 1976, 1977 (twice), 1978, 1979, 1980
ISBN 0 17 424257 3
NCN 0252 12 6

Phototypeset by Tradespools Ltd, Frome, Somerset

Printed in Hong Kong

We gratefully acknowledge the permission granted by:

Rupert Hart-Davies Ltd to reprint an extract from *The Drunken Forest* by Gerald Durrell.

George G. Harrap & Company Ltd to reprint an extract from *Anne of Green Gables* by L. M. Montgomery.

Parnassus Press Emeryville, California to reprint an extract from *A Wizard of Earthsea* by Ursula Le Guin.

Foreword

For the pupil being trained in the use of English, there are two modes of progression: one through speech and the other through writing. Each complements the other. The aim of this book is to secure the gradual development of the pupil's skill in both these aspects of language study.

In the writing of a story the pupil is faced with the exercise of framing mentally what he or she wants to say, of transferring these thoughts to paper, and of working in a medium which demands the use of punctuation. The material for written work has therefore been designed to give the pupil a sound grasp of sentence structure, to give practice in the setting down of thoughts in logical sequence, and to ensure a clear understanding of punctuation and its correct use. In story writing the pupil progresses from exercises based on narrative to those involving powers of description, explanation, and imagination.

The importance of the part played by good illustrative material in stimulating the pupil's mind and in heightening interest is acknowledged by the liberal use of this aid throughout the book.

The process of encouraging the pupil to use to good effect in oral work the skill gained in sentence structure and correct usage is one which demands all the teacher's skill and tact. The teacher has, on the one hand, to encourage the pupil to speak freely, and, on the other, to use what is said as a means of correcting and improving the style of expression. It is hoped that the varied exercises in the sections on oral work will prove helpful in this task by providing subject matter that is both interesting and within the range of the pupil's experience and observation.

Before you start

Your fourth book
This is your fourth English book. The lessons in it will take you in imagination to many interesting places – to a diamond mine in Africa, to tropical islands, to a nineteenth-century coaching-inn, to a quiet country village, and to the vastness of outer space. You will be asked to write stories of your own, and to speak about the things that interest you. To help you to do this, there are other lessons in which you will find certain rules for writing and speaking.

The correct way
Most boys and girls find that if they work hard, they can learn and remember these rules without any great difficulty. Having done so, they can then work in the correct way. They also find that it is just as easy to do things in the correct way as in the wrong way. It is essential, of course, to follow the rules both in speaking and in writing. When you write, the results are there on paper for your teacher or anyone else to see. When you speak, the results are heard by everyone around you.

Making use of words
As you work through this book, you will learn many new words. Try to make these words work for you. It is good to know the meaning of a word: it is even better to be able to use that word correctly in a sentence whenever you require it. Your dictionary is a great treasurehouse of words. Make as much use of it as possible.

Contents

1

Read this passage carefully:

> Bari's home was the monastery at the top of the St Bernard Pass which crosses the high, snow-clad Alps of Switzerland and leads into Italy. Bari was the best dog that the monks ever had. Famous for his rescue work, he had saved more lives than any other dog. When he died, the monks decided that their best dog would always be named Bari in memory of that wonderful animal. In the little chapel of the monastery there is a stained-glass window showing Bari with his red blanket strapped to his back, and his flask of brandy and packet of food tied to the front of his collar. He stands with his paw resting on the body of a traveller whom he has just dug out of the snow.

1 Now answer these questions, beginning your answer in each case with the underlined words:

- **a** What was Bari trained to do by the monks?
- **b** Give the reason why Bari had become famous.
- **c** What did he carry when he was at work?
- **d** What two countries are linked by the St Bernard Pass?
- **e** In what visible way is the memory of Bari kept alive?

2 Write your answers to the following questions:

- **a** Give the plural of monastery and the singular of lives.
- **b** What adjectives are formed from the nouns Switzerland and Italy?
- **c** Give four proper nouns from the above passage.
- **d** What two adjectives are used to describe the Alps?

3 Write this passage, putting in capital letters, full stops, and any other necessary punctuation marks:

the dog scraped vigorously to uncover the travellers body he then howled loudly to attract the monks attention they hurried with a stretcher to carry the traveller to the monastery of st bernard where he was cared for until he was well

4 Give two adverbs from the passage that you have just punctuated.

5 Punctuate the following:

ive told nancy that well meet at the corner of high street and bank street at five oclock said susan

6 Join the following pairs of sentences, using who, which, while, or until:

a We visited the monastery. It stands at the top of the Pass.
b A herd of goats passed the window. We were having breakfast.
c The dog wanders over the snow. It finds the scent of the buried person.
d The loud howls of the dog were heard by the monks. They were waiting anxiously at the monastery.

7 Complete the following sentences by means of suitable conjunctions:
a It was late evening ______________ we arrived at the Alpine village.
b ______________ we were tired, we did not sleep very soundly.
c They said that we would have to hurry ______________ we would be too late.
d We talked cheerfully ______________ we warmed ourselves at the fire.

8 Correct the following sentences. There are two errors in each.

a Jim and me is in the same class at school.
b I seen the too boys running away.
c Some of the girls has finished there work.
d Our friends told Laura and I that we had played good in the match.
e I asked if the dog had ate it's food.

9 Pair the words in the following list that are similar in meaning:

constable answer grumble risk trader careful sailor
choose solitude complain perilous reply sodden rival
policeman hazard behaviour alert opponent loneliness select
mariner conduct merchant cautious soaked dangerous watchful

10 Write the masculine nouns in the following list and opposite each put the feminine noun that matches it:

wife nephew waiter manageress husband waitress niece manager

2

1 Look at the pictures carefully and then write a story using the opening sentence given below. Thereafter try to build four sentences in the way shown, finishing your story in as interesting a way as possible.

One day, when he was out cycling, Jim Banks was amazed to find a car lying on its side at a bend in the road. He immediately ______________________________ and ____________________ but ______________________________________. Just as ____________________ he heard ______________________________________ from the foot of the slope. Quickly he ___________________________ to where _______________ lay.

"____________________ as soon as I can," he said to ________________________.

Now finish the story in your own way.

In the above story you wrote at least one sentence containing the two conjunctions and and but. Here are further examples showing how three short sentences can be joined by conjunctions.

a Nancy went outside. She played in the garden. Her friends came.
Nancy went outside and played in the garden until her friends came.

b We arrived home from school. We went straight to Dad's workshop. There we began work on the model.
When we arrived home from school, we went straight to Dad's workshop where we began work on the model.

Notice the following points:

a The underlined words are left out when the sentences are joined.

b In the second example one of the conjunctions is used at the beginning of the sentence. The introductory part of the sentence beginning with when is separated from the remainder of the sentence by a comma, thus:

When we arrived home from school, we ____________________.

2 Make one sentence out of each of these groups by using the conjunctions shown in the brackets:

a The fisherman landed the lobsters. He kept them in a big tank. It was time to send them to market. (and, until)
b The car drove on. They found a suitable hotel. There they could spend the night. (until, where)
c We went to the beach. We found a quiet spot. There we sat in the sun all afternoon. (when, where)
d Some of the crew searched the hold. Others searched the flight deck. They found no sign of the hijackers. (while, but)

Before the Fleming family went on holiday, Mrs Fleming asked her daughter Nancy to telephone Mr Brown the newsagent and cancel the delivery of newspapers while they were away. Nancy had also to ask Mr Brown to begin delivery on the day of their return. Nancy, who was in a hurry, said this on the telephone:

"Hello, Mr Brown. This is Nancy Fleming speaking. We are going on holiday soon and Mummy would like you to stop sending our newspapers while we are away. We would like you to begin again on the day we come back. Goodbye."

Why did Nancy's telephone message leave Mr Brown feeling very puzzled? Prepare the message you would have given Mr Brown, knowing, as Nancy did, that the holiday began on 3rd August and ended on 16th August.

3

Read this passage carefully:

> There are not many craftsmen left in the villages now, but in some parts of the country you will still find a special craft being practised as it has been done for hundreds of years. The women lace-makers of Honiton are an example of this, as are the weavers of the Hebrides who make the world-famous Harris tweed. But almost every village has its carpenter, who can make a good living, and there may still be a blacksmith in his forge. In the days when every farmer was dependent upon his horses both for working his fields and for transport for himself and his family, the smith was a very important man, and his craft is likely to be the oldest in the place. Perhaps he does not have to work so hard as his father did, but there is still plenty to do beside his main work of shoeing horses, for he is a useful man to mend a piece of machinery, or to make hinges for a country gate.
>
> (from *Country Scrap-Book for Boys and Girls* by Malcolm Saville)

1 Now answer these questions:

- **a** What craft is carried on in Honiton?
- **b** What other special craft is mentioned in the passage?
- **c** Give the name of a blacksmith's place of work.
- **d** Give one word that means hundreds of years.
- **e** Name a well known type of cloth mentioned in the passage.
- **f** Where do the makers of this cloth live?
- **g** What kind of work does a village blacksmith mostly do?
- **h** What other two jobs might he do?
- **i** What phrase in the brackets completes each sentence correctly?
  Villages have (few, a great many, no) craftsmen now.
  Blacksmiths were important when (none of, all, few of) the farmers kept horses.
  A village carpenter can earn (very little, a sufficient amount of, hardly any) money at his craft.
- **j** Name two tasks for which farmers needed horses.
- **k** Say whether the statements at the top of the next page are true or false.

1 The smith is always the oldest man in the village.
2 Farmers today no longer rely entirely on horses.
3 The smith now has to work much harder than his father did.
4 The village carpenter's life is one of poverty.
5 The blacksmith's importance declined as horses became fewer.
6 Very few villages nowadays have carpenters.

2 Which of the men or women mentioned in the passage would be likely to use the following?

chisel bellows loom anvil plane plough

3 Write the following words in a column: typewriter, hoe, safety-lamp, scissors, blow-lamp, compass, herbs, rifle, trowel, camera.

Opposite each of them write the name of the person from the list below who would be likely to use it:

barber	soldier	secretary	miner	bricklayer
cook	gardener	plumber	sailor	photographer

4 Here is a list of people and the tools and instruments they use. Find in your dictionary the meanings of any words you do not know.

awl	– cobbler	scalpel	– surgeon
baton	– conductor	telescope	– astronomer
goose	– tailor	plumb-line	– builder
palette	– artist	stethoscope	– doctor

5 Give one word for each of the following:

a a man born in Spain
b an Arab chief
c a hundred pence
d the fruit of an oak tree
e the boundary line between two countries
f an underwater vessel
g a spear to catch whales
h a shed where aircraft are kept

6 Explain clearly what the job of each of the following is:

nurse	chauffeur	journalist	cashier	judge
chemist	optician	lawyer	architect	warder

7 The following are shortened forms of longer words. Give in each case the longer word for: bus, exam, flu, gym, phone, photo, plane, pram.

4

In the following examples note carefully how commas are used when two or more nouns, adjectives, verbs, or adverbs come together in a sentence:

a At the airport we saw planes from America, Switzerland, France and Italy. (nouns)
b It was a fine, dry, cloudless day for flying. (adjectives)
c The customs officer examined, stamped and returned the passports. (verbs)
d The passengers' luggage was unloaded quickly, carefully and efficiently by the staff. (adverbs)

1 Write these sentences, putting the commas in the correct places:

a Matches were played at the Oval Old Trafford and Trent Bridge.
b From below decks came the slow steady muffled beat of the engines.
c The winger drove the ball suddenly swiftly and accurately into the net.
d The sculptor worked slowly skilfully and patiently at his task.
e Sledges drawn by horses reindeer or dogs were the only means of transport.

Note where commas are placed in the following sentences:

a In the canoe were two paddles, a short boat-hook and a towing line.
b The jet made its approach, glided in and touched down.

2 Now write these sentences, putting the commas in the correct places:

a A stamp album a pair of tweezers and a catalogue lay on the table.
b The wood used in the model must be quite dry well seasoned and free from knots.
c The man threw off his jacket dived into the water and brought the child to the bank.

3 Write this sentence, putting in the necessary capital letters:

the first man to swim the channel was captain webb who swam from dover to calais in 21 hours 45 minutes.

Nouns that are the names of males are said to be of the masculine gender, for example man, boy, bull, stag.

Nouns that are the names of females are said to be of the feminine gender, for example woman, girl, cow, hind.

Nouns that are the names of things without life are of the neuter gender, for example book, desk, table.

4 Nouns that may refer to either males or females are of the common gender, for example: child, parent.

Give the gender of the following nouns:

uncle	sister	friend	father	cousin	aunt	pencil	brother
cow	baby	window	mother	pupil	bull	duke	lady

5 Pair each masculine noun in List **a** with the feminine noun that matches it from List **b**:

a

mayor	drake	wizard	proprietor	earl	ram	baron
steward	gander	viscount	bachelor	buck	colt	prophet
landlord	nephew	stallion	bridegroom	marquis	host	boar

b

spinster	landlady	proprietress	bride	viscountess	witch	mare
mayoress	countess	stewardess	sow	niece	goose	doe
prophetess	hostess	marchioness	duck	baroness	filly	ewe

The words it's and its are often confused. The word it's is a shortened form of the two words it is. The word its means belonging to it.

Tom, it's time to go to bed. (it's = it is)
The dog has lost its collar. (its = belonging to it)

6 Write these sentences, putting it's or its in the spaces:

a ____________ a fine day.
b The plane returned to ____________ base.
c The bicycle lay on ____________ side.
d If ____________ going to rain, we shall stay indoors.
e ____________ now known that the yacht lost ____________ mast and foundered.
f The city is proud of ____________ ancient cathedral.
g The hurricane left a trail of damage in ____________ wake.

7 Write the following, choosing the correct word from the brackets:

(Too, two, to) of the party set (of, off) to join (there, their) friends.

5

1 The six pictures at the top of page 62 tell the story of how a lumberjack was saved by his dog. Study the pictures carefully and then tell the story in your own words.

2 Write a letter of thanks to a friend in a neighbouring town whose birthday party you attended last night, and enquire at the same time about a scarf which you think you may have left behind.

3 Draw an envelope in your exercise book and address it to your friend.

4 Arrange these sentences in order to make a short story. The third sentence of the story is marked for you.

In a short time the house was free of vermin.

The price of adult Siamese cats being high, they bought a female kitten.

They soon found that the house was overrun by rats and mice.

(3) On seeking advice, they were told to buy a Siamese cat.

Thereafter she worked steadily, killing mice by night and rats by day.

A young man and his wife once went to live in a farmhouse.

As soon as she had settled down in her new home, the kitten caught a rat as big as herself.

111 Briar Road
Faringdale
Surrey
4th February 1976

Please send me a copy of your list of Commonwealth stamps as advertised in Childrens Weekly

Tom Barnes

Here is a picture of a postcard. A postcard is a piece of thin cardboard measuring fourteen centimetres by nine centimetres, and is used for sending short messages. In this case Tom Barnes is asking for a list of stamps to be sent. Private messages should not be sent by postcard. Such messages should be sent by letter in a sealed envelope. Why?

Note that there are special rules about writing postcards.

a There is no greeting such as Dear Sir.
b Only the name of the writer is put at the end of the message.

The position of the address and the date is the same as in a letter.

5 Make one long sentence from each group of sentences below, using these conjunctions:

because until where although when and

- **a** Many parcels arrived for us. We were not allowed to open them before Christmas Day.
- **b** The old man had to stop and rest. His legs and back were aching.
- **c** Dad had read the morning paper. He put on his coat and hat. He went off to catch the bus.
- **d** Jim swam to the lilo. There he waited. I joined him.
- **e** The situation looked hopeless. They struggled on. They knew that to stop meant death.
- **f** Martin guarded the door. Terry watched from the window. I searched feverishly for the missing papers.
- **g** I became alarmed. I heard the noise of the train approaching. I was still far from the station.
- **h** The prospectors continued their journey. They reached a point in the river bed. There they found distinct traces of gold.

These pictures show some of the ways in which people enjoy themselves on holiday. If you have ever taken part in any of the holiday pastimes shown in the pictures, tell the class where you were at the time and what you were doing.

Imagine that you are being allowed to plan an ideal holiday. Prepare a short talk describing what kind of holiday you would plan, where you would spend it, and what you would do. Make a few notes on a piece of paper to help you when you speak.

Some people enjoy a holiday in the country and others a holiday at the seaside. Prepare a short talk explaining which type of holiday you prefer and give your reasons. Explain also why you do not like the other type of holiday.

6

The birds were in considerable numbers, sweeping round in great curves and circles at a uniform height of about two hundred and fifty feet from the surface. When fishing from that height, the gannet drops straight down on its prey, striking the sea with such force as to send up a column of water eight or ten feet high, the bird disappearing from sight for a space of five or six seconds, or longer, then after floating a few moments on the surface of the water, rising laboriously to resume its flight as before. The fall of the big white bird from such a height is a magnificent spectacle, and causes the spectator to hold his breath as he watches it with closed wings hurl itself down as if to certain perdition. The tremendous shock of the blow on the sea would certainly kill the bird but for the wad of dense elastic plumage which covers and protects it.

(from *The Land's End* by W. H. Hudson)

1 Now answer these questions:

a What bird is named in the passage?
b What two adjectives tell something about its size and colour?
c What prey does this type of bird seek?
d How long does it stay under the water?
e What word tells us that it does not rise easily and quickly from the surface of the water?
f Give two words from the passage that mean a wonderful sight.
g What prevents the bird from being killed as it hits the water?
h What verb suggests that the bird drops with tremendous speed?
i Give a word from the passage that means a person who watches.
j From what height do the birds drop?
k What does a person see when a bird hits the water?
l How would you change feet into metres?

2 From the adjective high we get the noun height. Form nouns from:

deep	strong	distant	wide	proud	just
brave	long	anxious	cruel	broad	hot

The opposites of the following verbs have been formed by adding a prefix, that is by adding certain letters to the beginning of the words:

verb:	appear	lock	behave
opposite:	disappear	unlock	misbehave

3 Write the opposites of these verbs by using the prefix dis, un, or mis:

fasten	agree	pack	mount	tie	lead
like	furl	use	do	fold	obey
embark	judge	arrange	lay	trust	understand

Now make sentences, using six of the words you have written.

4 Match the difficult words in **a** with the simpler meanings in **b**.

a velocity magnitude dexterity perdition descent altitude
b skill fall height speed ruin size

5 Which word does not belong to the group? Give a reason. The first one is done for you.

a bottle pail jug basket cup (all the others carry liquid)
b shirt shoes jacket coat vest
c cat donkey horse dog tiger
d coal iron copper zinc lead
e cub puppy chicken foal calf
f hours minutes seconds days clock
g trail path direction street road
h Bristol Leeds York Rome Birmingham
i sledge kayak canoe skiff boat
j wheat barley potatoes oats rye

6 Using a dictionary, an encyclopaedia, or other book of reference, divide the following in two groups: **a** sea-birds **b** land birds.

sparrow	guillemot	kittiwake	fulmar	eagle	albatross
thrush	herring gull	puffin	pheasant	nightingale	magpie

7 Complete the following. The first is done for you.

a Horse is to stable as dog is to kennel. (lawn, kennel, field)
b Uncle is to nephew as aunt is to ____________. (sister, mother, niece)
c Fish is to water as bird is to ____________. (air, wings, beak)
d Calf is to cow as foal is to ____________. (horse, mare, cub)

7

1 In the following sentences certain nouns are underlined. Give their kind (common or proper) and number (singular or plural).
In the match between Rockford and Swanleigh, Rockford's opening batsman scored a century. During his innings he hit twelve boundaries, and, as half of his team's wickets fell very quickly, became the hero of the match.

Plurals may be formed in the following ways:

		singular	**plural**
a	by adding s to the singular	wicket	wickets
b	by adding es when the singular ends in s, sh, ch, x, or o	match	matches
	(for exceptions, see A below)	hero	heroes
c	by changing the final y into i and adding es when the y comes after a consonant, or	century	centuries
	by adding s when y comes after a vowel	volley	volleys
d	by changing f or fe into v and adding es	half	halves
	(for exceptions, see B below)		
e	by changing the vowel sound	batsman	batsmen

A The following nouns ending in o add s to form the plural:

commando contralto curio dynamo memento photo
piano portfolio solo soprano studio tobacco

B The following nouns ending in f add s to form the plural:

chief cliff cuff dwarf grief gulf proof reef roof waif

Certain nouns have the same form in the singular and the plural:

brace (meaning a pair) deer dozen fish gross
grouse innings moose salmon score sheep trout

Certain nouns have no singular form. They are used only in the plural:

bellows dregs eaves measles news pliers
scissors spectacles suds thanks tongs tweezers trousers

2 Give the plural of: battery, chimney, echo, loaf, valley, piano, sheep, boundary, cliff, deer, lens, roof, torch, torpedo.

rule 1 When the subject of a sentence is singular, the verb must also be singular. When the subject is plural, the verb must be plural.

An umpire is the proper judge of fair or unfair play.
Umpires are the proper judges of fair or unfair play.

rule 2 When a sentence has two singular subjects joined by the word and, the verb must be plural.
The bat and ball were brand new.

rule 3 The following take singular verbs:

each	every	everybody	none	either of	anybody
each of	everyone	every one of	none of	neither of	nobody

3 Write the following, choosing the correct words from the brackets:

- **a** None of the girls (was, were) absent during the last fortnight.
- **b** Each of the players (was, were) tired at the end of the match.
- **c** The hat and coat (is, are) mine.
- **d** Neither of the films (was, were) good.
- **e** Each of the pupils (has, have) a book in which to write.
- **f** Anybody (is, are) welcome.
- **g** Everybody (was, were) happy at the holiday camp.
- **h** Either of them (is, are) willing to do the job.
- **i** Bob and Susan (has, have) come to spend Christmas with us.
- **j** (Is, Are) either of the twins here?
- **k** Neither of the boys (has, have) won although each of them (was, were) trying his best.
- **l** Each drawing (was, were) examined but none (was, were) good enough.
- **m** Every one of the events (was, were) good and nobody (was, were) disappointed.
- **n** Every part of the fields (was, were) searched but none of the money (was, were) found.

4 Write the following, putting the apostrophe in the correct place:

- **a** The drivers name and the cars number were noted in the policemans book.
- **b** The shop window contained girls dresses and childrens coats.
- **c** The boys bicycles were repaired at Mr. Wilsons garage.
- **d** The hotels car park was full of travellers cars.

5 Write the following, putting in commas, apostrophes, question marks, and inverted commas where necessary:

- **a** youll find the task long difficult and dangerous said major gray.
- **b** the men replied we are still willing to volunteer.
- **c** when do we set off asked one of them.
- **d** as soon as its dark answered the major.

8

1 Arrange these sentences in proper order to compose a story about *Training a Puppy*. The third sentence of the story is marked.

The puppy can then be taken into the garden.
The first thing to do is to accustom it to wearing a collar.
(3) This sometimes takes a little time.
When a puppy is about six months old, its training should begin.
There it will probably try to chew through the lead and run off.
A very light lead can then be attached to the collar.

2 Form the opposite of each of these words by adding the prefix in, un, im, dis, or mis:

justice	fortune	popular	correct	sincere
polite	courtesy	suitable	important	patient
inform	please	convenient	place	

3 With what person do you associate the following?

baton wig awl palette stethoscope

4 Complete each phrase below with a suitable adjective from this list:

remorseless	quaint	nimble
prominent	superior	favourable

a __________ custom   with __________ feet   a __________ enemy
a __________ landmark   a __________ report   of __________ quality

5 Make one long sentence by joining each of these groups of sentences:

a Helen was eleven years old. She had to go to the local comprehensive school by train. The school was a long way from her home.
b The pond had frozen over. We could not go skating. The ice was not yet strong enough to bear our weight.
c The lady was coming out of the Post Office. She had been buying stamps. She dropped her purse.

6 Complete the following sentences by using the conjunctions unless, after, until, and as:

a __________ the storm had died down, the telephone engineers worked without a break __________ they had repaired all the damaged lines.
b __________ we were letting our dog off its lead, the park keeper advised us not to __________ the dog was properly trained.

7 Divide the group of nouns below into Masculine, Feminine, Common, Neuter.

hostess	nephew	friend	book	infant	bachelor
earl	spinster	picture	cousin	desk	bride

8 Divide the following sentence into subject and predicate, and then answer the questions given below:

Our visitor from New York arrived safely at Heathrow yesterday.

- **a** Give a common noun from the above sentence.
- **b** What is the gender of the noun you have written?
- **c** Write a proper noun from the sentence.
- **d** What is the verb in the sentence?
- **e** Write an adverb from the sentence.

9 Write the following passage, putting in the necessary capital letters, commas, and full stops:

the police are most useful members of our community they keep order in the streets direct the traffic guard our property and come to the rescue when there is an accident more than a hundred years ago sir robert peel decided that there should be a band of men trained for police duties parliament made a law ordering this to be done and the first london policeman began work in 1829

10 Choose the correct words from the brackets to complete each sentence:

- **a** The books (was, were) given out and the pupils began (there, their) hymn practice
- **b** (To, too, two) of the questions were about maps but neither of them (was, were) difficult.
- **c** The teacher told Terry and (I, me) to write (neat, neatly).
- **d** Tell me when (its, it's) time to go to the kennel to give the dog (its, it's) meal.

11 Form adjectives from these nouns:

mountain	help	gold	winter
comfort	month	hero	absence

9

The Coral Island, written by R. M. Ballantyne, tells of the adventures of three boys, Ralph, Jack, and Peterkin, who were cast ashore on an uninhabited island in the Pacific Ocean. Their ship, the *Arrow*, had struck a reef during a storm and foundered immediately. Only the boys reached the shore. The pictures show some of the exciting events related in the book. Study these scenes and then answer the questions below.

1

2

3

4

- **a** How did the boys manage to reach the shore?
- **b** What kind of climate do you think the island had. Why?
- **c** Give two reasons why the trees in the second picture would be important to the boys.
- **d** What are the boys trying to do in picture 3?
- **e** Can you explain how this can be done with the materials shown?
- **f** What type of fish is shown in the fourth picture? How can you tell?

The Swiss Family Robinson, written by Johann Wyss, tells how a family of six – the father, mother, and four boys – suffered shipwreck on a voyage to America, after being driven south-eastward by a terrible storm. When the ship struck, the crew took to the boats, leaving the family who were below-decks to their fate. Next morning, when the storm had abated, the ship was still firmly wedged on some rocks at no great distance from an island.

a How did the family solve the problem of leaving the ship together?

b They later returned to rescue the animals that were on board. How did they ensure that the animals would reach the shore safely?

c Explain why these animals would prove valuable to the family.

d What are the family doing in picture 3? Why are they doing this?

e You see a rope ladder in position. How do you think they set about achieving this? There is a clue in the picture.

f After removing all useful material from the ship the father decided to make further use of it. Look at picture 4 and explain what he did.

g In what way were the Robinsons luckier than the boys stranded on Coral Island?

10

These pictures tell the story of how a boy named Tony Morris almost found himself in trouble because he was trying to be helpful. Luckily for him, the girl who was sitting on the deck chair saw all that happened and was able to help him.

1 If you are a boy, imagine that you are Tony Morris. Tell the story as if it had happened to you. If you are a girl, imagine that you are the girl in the deck chair. Tell what you saw and explain how you were able to help.

In Book 3 you learned how to join sentences by using the words who and which.
We joined the charity marchers. They were going on a sponsored walk.
We joined the charity marchers who were going on a sponsored walk.

I found the keys. I lost them a week ago.
I found the keys which I lost a week ago.

Who is used when referring to people, and which when referring to things.

In the examples on the previous page the word who or which was placed at the end of the first sentence when the two sentences were joined. If you study the following examples carefully, you will see that it is not always possible to join the sentences in exactly that way.

The burglar was sentenced to one year's imprisonment by the judge. He had three previous convictions.

The burglar, who had three previous convictions, was sentenced to one year's imprisonment by the judge.

If you were to join these two sentences without first thinking carefully, you would produce this rather strange sentence:

The burglar was sentenced to one year's imprisonment by the judge who had three previous convictions.

rule Always place who or which as near as possible to the word to which it refers.

2 Join the following sentences, using who or which:

a The boy fell off his bicycle. He brings us our newspapers.
b The man carried a large parcel. He sat down beside us.
c The man was arrested next day. He stole my sister's purse.
d The lion was soon captured. It had escaped from the zoo.
e The gale tore down a TV aerial. It sprang up during the night.

The six pictures on the bottom half of page 62 deal with lumbering in Canada. Study these pictures, making any brief notes you wish, and be prepared to explain clearly how and at what seasons of the year the timber travels on the various stages of its journey from the forest to the sawmill.

Imagine that a water pipe has burst in your house and that you are making a telephone call to ask the plumber to come as soon as possible. What would you say?

Give a short talk to explain clearly the difference between:

a a river and a canal
b a helicopter and an aeroplane
c television and the cinema
d a lift and an escalator
e a dry cleaner's and a laundry

11

Read this passage carefully:

> "Now, sir, time to get up, if you please. Tally-ho coach for Leicester will be round in half an hour." So spake the boots of the Peacock Inn, Islington, at half past two on the morning of a day in the early part of November 183–, giving Tom Brown at the same time a shake by the shoulder, and carrying off his shoes to clean. Tom and his father arrived in town from Berkshire the day before, and finding, on inquiry, that the Birmingham coaches which ran from the city did not pass through Rugby but deposited their passengers at Dunchurch, a village three miles distant on the main road, had resolved that Tom should travel down by the Tally-ho, which diverged from the main road and passed through Rugby.
>
> (from *Tom Brown's Schooldays* by Thomas Hughes)

1 Now answer these questions:

a In what season of the year was this journey being made?
b What was the name of the coach in which Tom was to travel?
c At what time was it due to leave the Peacock Inn?
d To what town was Tom Brown travelling?
e Did the Leicester coach pass through Rugby?
f What was the final destination of the coach on which Tom was to travel?
g Which place was <u>not</u> on the main road? (Dunchurch, Islington, Rugby)
h Name two duties of the boots at the Peacock Inn.
i Where were the passengers for Rugby put down by the Birmingham coach? (Islington, Dunchurch, Leicester)
j What does the word <u>diverged</u> mean? (galloped, turned off, slowed down)
k Where had Tom come from on the previous day?

2 Pair each verb in line **a** with one of opposite meaning from line **b**.

a	flow	allow	expand	owe	defend	descend
b	attack	repay	ascend	ebb	forbid	contract

3 Pick out from each line two adjectives that are similar in meaning:

a	fierce	perilous	bold	hazardous	strong
b	abundant	crowded	stormy	rich	plentiful
c	powerful	heavy	hostile	unfriendly	bright
d	tranquil	weak	peaceful	idle	deep
e	strange	anxious	vague	annual	yearly
f	feeble	cautious	timid	careful	dreary

4 Write these sentences, using in each case a verb of similar meaning to replace the underlined verb:

a Next day we <u>encountered</u> the enemy.
b The thief <u>concealed</u> the jewels.
c The paper <u>adhered</u> to my fingers.
d The guard <u>liberated</u> the prisoners.
e We <u>purchased</u> food at the shop.
f The king <u>governed</u> wisely.
g Sandra <u>imitated</u> her sister.
h He <u>toppled</u> into the water.
i The lady <u>notified</u> the police.
j A great crowd <u>assembled</u>.

5 Use your dictionary if necessary to find the answers to the following. The answers are arranged in alphabetical order.

a a large Spanish sailing ship of long ago g_l_ _ _ _
b an African animal with a long neck g_r_ _ _ _
c a man paid to fight in the arenas of ancient Rome g_a_ _ _ _ _ _
d a type of boat used on the canals of Venice g_n_ _ _ _
e a Dutch silver coin g_i_ _ _ _
f an old English coin worth twenty-one shillings g_i_ _ _

6 Here is a table showing the dates on which certain films were shown at three cinemas. Study the table and answer the questions below.

	9th March	**16th March**	**23rd March**
Ritz	Casablanca	The Petrified Forest	The Maltese Falcon
Rio	Key Largo	The Maltese Falcon	To Have and Have Not
Savoy	The Maltese Falcon	The Big Sleep	Key Largo

a What film was shown at the Rio on 23rd March?
b In what cinema was *The Maltese Falcon* shown on 9th March?
c On what date did the Ritz show *The Petrified Forest*?

12

A noun that is used to name a group of persons, animals, or things is called a collective noun. These nouns in italics are collective nouns:

a crowd of people   a gang of thieves   a team of players

1 Choose a collective noun from this list to complete each phrase below:

flight	brood	troop	clutch	range
suite	school	clump	choir	sheaf

a a ____________ of trees
b a ____________ of eggs
c a ____________ of steps
d a ____________ of whales
e a ____________ of corn
f a ____________ of mountains
g a ____________ of monkeys
h a ____________ of furniture
i a ____________ of chickens
j a ____________ of singers

2 Complete each of these phrases with a suitable word:

a a bunch of ____________
b a swarm of ____________
c a herd of ____________
d a fleet of ____________
e a library of ____________
f a flock of ____________
g a shoal of ____________
h a squad of ____________
i a board of ____________
j a plague of ____________

A sentence which contains only one subject and one predicate is called a simple sentence. In the following simple sentences the subject in each case is underlined. Note that the subject is not always at the beginning of the sentence.

a My best friend lives next door.
b We sailed along the canal.
c The ball soared over the wall.
d Into the valley of Death rode the six hundred.
e The man in the blue uniform spoke to the passengers.

3 Divide the following sentences into subject and predicate:

a The nurse attended to the patients.
b I went to the nearest village.
c A rumble of thunder broke the silence.

d Over the spot hovered the rescue helicopter.
e At the corner of the street stood an old shop.
f The crew of the space ship checked all the controls.

A full stop is used after abbreviated words and the initials of a person's name. These examples show some commonly used abbreviations:

Professor Thomas Robert Pearson	Prof. T. R. Pearson
Reverend John Frederick Hill	Rev. J. F. Hill
John Anderson Brown and Company Limited	J. A. Brown and Co. Ltd
On Her Majesty's Service	O.H.M.S.

But often when the last letter of the contraction is the same as the last letter of the word we leave out the full stop. For example: Doctor, Dr

4 Write the following in abbreviated form:

a Miss Elizabeth Ann Jackson
b General Post Office
c Royal Air Force
d Member of Parliament
e Justice of the Peace
f British Broadcasting Corporation
g European Economic Community
h Her Royal Highness
i United States of America
j Before Christ
k Alexander Charles Trent and Company Limited, 14 Shore Street

The names of months, except May, June, and July, may be abbreviated thus:

January – Jan.	April – Apr.	October – Oct.
February – Feb.	August – Aug.	November – Nov.
March – Mar.	September – Sept.	December – Dec.

Singular subjects separated by either . . . or or neither . . . nor take a singular verb. Plural subjects separated in this way take a plural verb. Note the verbs in the following examples:

a Either the one or the other is sure to come.
Neither the boy nor his sister knows what happened.

b Either the children or their friends are playing a trick.
Neither the boys nor the girls have finished the exercise.

5 Write the following sentences, choosing the correct verb from the brackets:

a Either the fog or the snow (has, have) delayed the bus.
b Neither the shops nor the cinemas (is, are) open today.
c If either the butcher or the milkman (calls, call) let me know.
d He says that neither the watch nor the ring (has, have) been found.
e We asked if either the monkeys or the elephants (was, were) on show.

13

Here is a picture of a room:

You can see at once that it has not been looked after very well. Let us imagine that you are writing a letter to a friend, describing a visit to such a room. You might write in this way:

When I entered the room, I was shocked by its appearance. A heap of old newspapers, boots, and clothing lay on the dirty floor. Faded wallpaper hung in strips from the wall, and in the ceiling a gaping hole showed where some of the plaster had fallen down. Although the day was bright outside, only a little light came through the layer of dust and cobwebs which covered the curtainless window. The furniture consisted of an old bed, two broken chairs, and a grimy chest of drawers.

Notice the following points:

a The various parts of the room are described in orderly fashion:
(1) floor (2) walls (3) ceiling (4) window (5) furniture

b Many adjectives – old, dirty, faded, broken, etc. – are used to give the reader an exact picture of what is seen.

c Commas are used when lists of things are mentioned, and in sentences beginning with the conjunctions when and although.

This is a picture of a very different kind of room. Write a description of it.

Before you begin, think carefully of (1) the order in which you are going to describe the various parts of the room, (2) the adjectives that will best give your reader an exact picture of what you see, and (3) the different ways in which you can vary the structure of your sentences to prevent your description from becoming monotonous.

1 Read the following, noting how each pair of sentences is joined:

a We spoke to the actor. We met him backstage.
We spoke to the actor whom we met backstage.

b I was thanked by the old lady. I had directed her to the station.
I was thanked by the old lady whom I had directed to the station.

The joining word is whom. Note that in the second sentence of each pair the pronouns him and her are left out when the sentences are joined.

2 Now join these sentences in the way shown above:

- **a** The pilot was thanked by the passengers. He had brought the damaged plane down safely
- **b** We visited the Smiths. We had met them on holiday.
- **c** The soldiers fought well under their general. They respected and admired him.
- **d** She is a friend. I have her staying with me for the weekend.
- **e** The groundsman chased the boys. He had found them playing football on the the cricket pitch.

The following example will show that the word whom must always be placed as near as possible to the word to which it refers.

The leader of the gang was caught. We had recognised him.
The leader of the gang whom we had recognised was caught.

3 Join these sentences, using whom:

- **a** Our new neighbours invited me to tea. I like them very much.
- **b** That man is very famous. I pointed him out.
- **c** The singer from London gave us her autograph. We have often seen her on TV.
- **d** The sailors were given dry clothes. We rescued them.
- **e** Our friends have not failed us. We trusted them completely.

Choose any one of the following items and say how you would describe it exactly to the clerk at a railway lost property office if you had left it on a train:

- **a** your mother's shopping bag
- **b** your hat
- **c** your coat
- **d** your hamster
- **e** your scarf
- **f** your purse

14

Read this passage carefully:

Presently a light step sounded on the stairs and somebody entered the room.

"Oh, Marilla," sobbed Anne without looking up, "I'm disgraced for ever. I shall never be able to live this down. It will get out – things always do get out in Avonlea. Diana will ask me how my cake turned out and I shall have to tell her the truth. I shall always be pointed at as the girl who flavoured a cake with anodyne liniment. Gil – the boys in school will never get over laughing at it. Oh, Marilla, if you have a spark of Christian pity don't tell me that I must go down and wash the dishes after this. I'll wash them when the minister and his wife are gone, but I cannot ever look Mrs Allan in the face again. Perhaps she'll think I tried to poison her. Mrs Lynde says she knows an orphan girl who tried to poison her benefactor. But the liniment isn't poisonous. It's meant to be taken internally – although not in cakes. Won't you tell Mrs Allan so, Marilla?"

"Suppose you jump up and tell her so yourself," said a merry voice.

Anne flew up, to find Mrs Allan standing by her bed, surveying her with laughing eyes.

"My dear little girl, you mustn't cry like this," she said, genuinely disturbed by Anne's tragic face. "Why, it's all just a funny mistake that anybody might make."

"Oh, no, it takes me to make such a mistake," said Anne forlornly, "And I wanted to have that cake so nice for you, Mrs Allan."

(From *Anne of Green Gables*
by L. M. Montgomery)

1 Now answer the following questions. Begin your answer with the words that have been underlined.

a Who was <u>the person who came into Anne's room</u>?

b With what had <u>Anne</u> flavoured the cake?

c Was the liniment poisonous?
d How was the liniment meant to be taken?
e Why did Anne feel she could never look Mrs Allan in the face again?
f What is the meaning of benefactor?
g What is the meaning of liniment?
h What is the meaning of tragic?

2 Make adjectives from the following nouns. The first is done for you.

interest (interesting) courage success profit year tropics science

Certain words in our language have the same pronunciation but are different in meaning and in spelling. Here are some examples of such words used in sentences:

a We gathered seaweed on the beach.
b That is a beech tree.
c I bought this bicycle at a sale.
d He hoisted the sail of the boat.

3 Write the sentences given below, choosing for each space the correct word from this list:

pane	chews	peeled	sent	current	grate
pain	choose	pealed	scent	currant	great

a The bell ______ loudly.
b The ______ swept him downstream.
c The hounds lost the ______.
d The fire burned in the ______.
e I had to ______ the school team.
f The ball broke one ______ of glass.

4 Write sentences using the following words correctly:

new	hole	piece	guest	course	peer
knew	whole	peace	guessed	coarse	pier

5 Find from your dictionary the difference between the following:

stationary	cord	choir	isle	assent	principle
stationery	chord	quire	aisle	ascent	principal

6 Complete the following. The first is done for you.

a Kitten is to cat as puppy is to dog. (kennel, dog, mouse)
b Ear is to hearing as eye is to ______. (glass, window, seeing)
c Green is to grass as ______ is to daffodil. (blue, yellow, red)
d Farmer is to land as fisherman is to ______. (sea, wind, sky)
e Hat is to ______ as shoe is to foot. (face, eyes, head)

7 Place the following words into three groups and give each group a name:

fish	coat	cottage	stockings	house	cheese
hat	gloves	meat	caravan	bread	bungalow

15

FAST FASTER FASTEST

When talking about the speed of the car and the bicycle shown above, it would be correct to say that the car was faster than the bicycle. Similarly, when talking about the three objects shown, it would be correct to say that the plane was the fastest of the three.

We speak of the faster of two things, and the fastest of three or more.

Adjectives are compared in the following way. There are three degrees of comparison:

positive	**comparative**	**superlative**
fast	faster	fastest
hot	hotter	hottest
happy	happier	happiest
good	better	best
bad	worse	worst

In most adjectives of two syllables and in all adjectives of more than two syllables the comparative is formed by adding more and the superlative by adding most to the positive form. (A syllable is a part of a word that can be pronounced as a single sound. For example, the word fast has one syllable, the word beau-ti-ful three.)

positive	**comparative**	**superlative**
beautiful	more beautiful	most beautiful
famous	more famous	most famous
curious	more curious	most curious

In your speech and writing do not be guilty of errors such as these:

This hill is more steeper than the other one. (wrong)
He was the most bravest man of them all. (wrong)

1 Draw a table of three columns with the headings positive, comparative, and superlative and fill in your table for these adjectives:

kind	early	furious	wonderful	strong
thin	keen	clumsy	honest	eager

A long spoken sentence may, when written, be put down in two ways. Notice where the commas are placed in each example.

"We went to the shop and chose a present for Mum," said Nancy.
"We went to the shop," said Nancy, "and chose a present for Mum."

2 Punctuate the following sentences:

a I finished my homework and then watched TV said Nancy.
b When we visited the docks said Tom we saw big ships being loaded.
c Go to the next crossing said the policeman and turn right.
d Well have tea early tonight and go to the cinema said Dad.

3 Write the following, putting in the necessary capitals and full stops:

a great crowd had assembled near darlington in durham they had come to see the opening of the first steam railway in the world the engine had been built by george stephenson many people had come expecting to see it blow up in front of it went a horseman with a flag his job was to warn people off the line stephenson himself was the engine driver

4 Rewrite these sentences correctly. Can you spot two mistakes in **e**?

a Jim is undoubtedly the better runner of the three.
b This is the fastest of the two trains.
c Of the four books this is the more interesting.
d Of the two teams ours was the best.
e Robert took the biggest half of the apple.

Note carefully how to use such phrases as older than . . . , taller than . . . , as old as . . . , as tall as . . . , etc.

My brother is older than I (am). (correct)
My brother is older than me. (wrong)
Tom is as old as I (am). (correct)
Tom is as old as me. (wrong)

16

1 These two pictures are taken from different stories. Each shows the point at which the story becomes very exciting. Choose the picture which interests you the more. Write a story telling what led up to the event shown in the picture and finish the composition in your own way.

2 A very severe storm breaks. Houses in a village are flooded, and a farm building near the village is struck by lightning and set on fire. The villagers rush to help the farmer to rescue the animals and to put out the fire. One boy later wrote a story about the storm. This is what he wrote:

There was a storm in our village yesterday. It rained hard. Lightning struck a barn. The roads were covered with water. It was terrible.

Discuss what he wrote and say how he could have made it more interesting. When you have done so, write a story yourself which gives a much clearer account of what actually happened.

3 Improve these sentences by using who or which in place of and:

- **a** The prize was won by a man and he lived in Leeds.
- **b** I gave the prescription to the chemist and the doctor had written it.
- **c** The girl sprained her ankle and she was running for the bus.
- **d** The lorry was out of control and it hit the lamp-post.
- **e** History is very interesting and we learn about it at school.
- **f** The boy was praised by the police and he discovered the fire.

The following sentences have been joined by the word whose:

He is a brilliant scientist. His fame has spread across the world.
He is a brilliant scientist whose fame has spread across the world.

The word whose, which replaces his in the above sentence, can also be used to take the place of the words her or their. It is not always possible to put the joining word whose at the end of the first sentence as we did above. Whose, like the joining words who, which, and whom, must always be placed as near as possible to the word to which it refers.

The rescue party were exhausted. Their efforts had saved many lives.
The rescue party whose efforts had saved many lives were exhausted.

4 Join the following sentences by the word whose, making certain that it is placed as near as possible to the word to which it refers:

a This is the boy. His book was lost.
b The girls are staying with us. Their parents are abroad.
c She is a kind lady. Her life is spent in helping others.
d The author was born in this town. You have read his book.
e The witness was complimented by the judge. His evidence was given very clearly.
f A new boy joined our class today. His father is a pilot.
g Great interest was aroused by the story of the young men. Their adventures had so stirred the imagination of the public.

5 Study this table of charges for parcels and then answer the questions below:

Weight	Distance (in kilometres)			
kg	up to 30	31–50	51–100	over 100
5	63p	65p	68p	70p
10	95p	98p	100p	103p
15	101p	104p	107p	109p

a What is the cost of sending a 15-kg parcel over 100 kilometres?
b How far can a parcel of 10 kg be sent for 98p
c What weight of parcel could be sent 40 kilometres for 104p?

Jim Cook's father arranged to meet him at a certain place after school. This is what Jim had to do. He had to walk from the school to High Street, cross at the traffic lights, and turn right. He had then to go to the café which was next to the old cinema and wait there for his father. Imagine that you are Jim's father. Without looking at your book more than once again, be prepared to give the above instructions to Jim, beginning with the words "When you come out of school . . ."

17

Read this passage carefully:

He kept his course to the southeast, and the land sank out of sight as night came over the eastern edge of the world. The hollows of the waves all were full of darkness while the crests shone yet with a clear ruddy reflection of the west. Ged sang aloud the Winter Carol and such cantos of the *Deed of the Young King* as he remembered, for those songs are sung at the Festival of Sunreturn. His voice was clear but it fell to nothing in the vast silence of the sea. Darkness came quickly and the winter stars.

All that longest night of the year he waked, watching the stars rise upon his left hand and wheel overhead and sink into far black waters on the right, while always the long wind of winter bore him southward over an unseen sea. He could sleep for only a moment now and then, with a sharp awakening. This boat he sailed was in truth no boat but a thing more than half charm and sorcery, and the rest of it mere planks and driftwood which, if he let slack the shaping-spells and the binding-spell upon them, would soon enough lapse and scatter and go drifting off as a little flotsam on the waves. The sail too, woven of magic and the air, would not long stay against the wind if he slept, but would turn to a puff of wind itself. Ged's spells were cogent and potent, but when the matter on which such spells work is small, the power that keeps them working must be renewed from moment to moment: so he slept not that night. He would have gone easier and swifter as falcon or dolphin, but Ogion had advised him not to change his shape, and he knew the value of Ogion's advice. So he sailed southward under the west-going stars, and the long night passed slowly, until the first day of the new year brightened all the sea.

(from *A Wizard of Earthsea* by Ursula le Guin)

1 Now answer these questions:

a What materials had Ged used in making his boat?
b Which two songs did Ged sing?

c At which festival were these songs usually sung?
d What season of the year was it when Ged made his journey?
e On which side of Ged did the stars rise?
f In which direction was he sailing?
g Who had advised him not to change his shape?
h Why did Ged not sleep during the night?
i Use your dictionary to find the meaning of cogent, potent, and flotsam.
j Write the words from the passage which mean: (1) verses, (2) huge, (3) disperse.

The underlined phrases in the following sentences are called similes. In a simile we say that a person or thing is like another.

a Mary was as busy as a bee.
b Dick was as hungry as a hunter.
c The room was as clean as a new pin.
d The boy was as white as a ghost.

2 Use these words to complete the similes below:

judge	rock	fiddle	velvet	mouse
bell	eel	king	peacock	flounder

a as timid as a ______________
b as happy as a ______________
c as slippery as an ______________
d as sober as a ______________
e as proud as a ______________
f as flat as a ______________
g as smooth as ______________
h as fit as a ______________
i as steady as a ______________
j as sound as a ______________

3 Complete each of the similes below with an adjective from this list:

fresh	clear	wise	bold	keen
good	strong	dull	cool	stiff

a as ______________ as mustard
b as ______________ as a poker
c as ______________ as an ox
d as ______________ as gold
e as ______________ as brass
f as ______________ as paint
g as ______________ as crystal
h as ______________ as a cucumber
i as ______________ as an owl
j as ______________ as ditchwater

18

1 Arrange these sentences in proper order to make a short story about *Kites*. The third sentence of the story is marked for you.

They have contributed in the past to scientific research.
Kites were known to the Chinese at a very early date.
(3) Kites, however, can be regarded as more than just fascinating toys.
For such serious work the box kite was usually chosen because of its great lifting power and stability.
They were flown by them and other eastern nations on festive occasions.

2 Write four short sentences, using each of the following words once:

frequent happiest stationary extinguish

3 Complete each of these phrases with a suitable word:

a regiment of ____________	a ____________ of rubbish
a string of ____________	a ____________ of flowers
a bench of ____________	a ____________ of birds
a clump of ____________	a ____________ of herring
a range of ____________	a ____________ of furniture

4 Write the following abbreviations in full:

a B.B.C. O.H.M.S. R.A.F. R.N. M.P. G.P.O. B.C.
b Thos. Brookes & Co. Ltd, 207 Union St.
c Feb. Aug. Nov. Rev. Dr

5 Write these words and opposite each give another word which sounds the same but is spelt differently:

scent	pealed	way	root	stake
key	pray	told	waste	paws

6 Join the following sentences by who, which, whom, or whose:

a The little girl is broken-hearted. Her puppy is lost.
b The visitors did not arrive. We were expecting them.
c The Pyramids are the tombs of Egyptian kings and queens. They rise in the desert to the east of Cairo.
d The pupil was praised by the teacher. She did her best.
e My friend has to walk to school. His bicycle was damaged.

7 Choose from each line two adjectives that are opposite in meaning:

a	wise	proud	kind	humble	brave
b	good	lovely	rare	perfect	common
c	legal	correct	proper	illegal	risky
d	ugly	bad	diligent	lazy	bitter
e	wide	solid	foolish	small	sensible

8 Write in a column the underlined verbs and opposite each give a verb of similar meaning:

- **a** We were able to observe the animals at close quarters.
- **b** The ship vanished without trace.
- **c** The boy trembled with fright.
- **d** Cycling is prohibited on the footpath.
- **e** The crowd implored their team to score another goal.
- **f** The holidaymakers sauntered along the beach.
- **g** The sound engineer spliced the ends of the tape.
- **h** The mouse scurried away from the cat.
- **i** The noise aroused the sleeping giant.
- **j** The school term commenced last Thursday.

9 Compare the following adjectives:

wide precious hot merry plentiful narrow

10 Pair each noun in list **a** with one of similar meaning from list **b**:

a: swamp race calamity courage malady
b: illness fortitude disaster nation marsh

11 Correct the following sentences:

- **a** Neither Mark nor his sister are at school today.
- **b** Each of the shelves were filled with books.
- **c** Helen's sister is older than me.
- **d** My father and me went to the football match.
- **e** "Which of the two teams was the best?"

12 Punctuate these sentences:

- **a** Come with me said the farmer and I will show you the lambs
- **b** I ran all the way said Tania but I missed the bus

19

You have already seen how it is possible to improve sentences by the careful choice of adjectives, verbs, and adverbs. You have also learned how to improve sentences by the use of similes. Look now at the phrases underlined in the following sentences:

- **a** We searched high and low for the missing ring.
- **b** Everything in the house was spick and span.
- **c** The dogs fought tooth and nail for the scraps of food.

The use of such phrases adds force to our sentences.

1 Use these phrases to complete the sentences below:

lock and key	wear and tear	all and sundry
beck and call	high and dry	ups and downs

- **a** The ship was left ________________ by the ebbing tide.
- **b** ________________ joined in the fun.
- **c** The car stood up well to the ________________ of the rough journey
- **d** The valuables were placed safely under ________________.
- **e** During his long life the old man had many ________________.
- **f** The overworked waitress was at everyone's ________________.

2 Complete each phrase with a word chosen from this list:

ends soul cry hearty sound means

hue and ____________	heart and ____________
safe and ____________	ways and ____________
odds and ____________	hale and ____________

Three of the most overworked words in our language are get, got, and nice. You will find below lists of words which can be used in place of these words. Study these lists and refer to them when you feel tempted to use get, got, or nice:

get (a present)	– receive	get (on)	– board
get (cold)	– become	get (out)	– alight
get (a cold)	– catch	get (away)	– escape
get (slippers)	– fetch		
get (breakfast)	– eat	nice (dress)	– pretty
get (together)	– collect	nice (voice)	– pleasant
get (ready)	– prepare	nice (holidays)	– enjoyable
get (up)	– rise	nice (weather)	– fine
get (to)	– reach	nice (story)	– interesting
get (in)	– arrive	nice (flowers)	– lovely
get (off)	– dismount	nice (view)	– beautiful

The following examples show how it is possible to say something in a number of different ways:

a Andrew climbed up the ladder but found that he could not reach the ball.
b Although Andrew climbed to the top of the ladder, he found that he could not reach the ball.
c When he climbed to the top of the ladder, Andrew found that he could not reach the ball.

3 Join the following sentences in at least two different ways:

Simon made a desperate effort towards the end of the race. He found that his opponent could still maintain his lead.

4 In our speech we often use sayings which contain in a few words some well-known truth or moral lesson. Such sayings are called proverbs. Read the following proverbs and then choose the sentence from the list below that explains the meaning of each.

Make hay while the sun shines.
Still waters run deep.
Once bitten, twice shy.
A stitch in time saves nine.
Birds of a feather flock together.
The least said the soonest mended.
New brooms sweep clean.
Let sleeping dogs lie.

a Do not deliberately stir up trouble.
b It is wise to say very little.
c Having been once injured, a person takes care to avoid danger in the future.
d People newly appointed to their jobs are inclined to make changes.
e Always take advantage of an opportunity when it arises.
f Action taken promptly prevents greater misfortune befalling you.
g Quiet people are usually very profound thinkers.
h A person is known by the company he or she keeps.

5 Sometimes one proverb seems to cancel another. Say which of the following do so:

a Absence makes the heart grow fonder.
b Too many cooks spoil the broth.
c Many hands make light work.
d Out of sight, out of mind.

20

Note the underlined words in the following sentences:

- **a** He put the parcel on the table.
- **b** The train came from Bristol.
- **c** The boy sat under the tree.
- **d** The lady was kind to children.

The underlined words are called prepositions. A preposition is a word placed before a noun or a pronoun to show in what relation one thing stands to another. Here are some commonly used prepositions:

above across after among at before behind below beside between by down for from in into near of off on over round through to under up with

1 Complete each sentence with a suitable preposition:

- **a** The cat slept ______________ the chair.
- **b** We played games ______________ tea.
- **c** The boy swam ______________ the river.
- **d** He carried the bag ______________ us.
- **e** She hid the book ______________ the chair.
- **f** The ship sailed ______________ the bay.
- **g** The dog ran ______________ the field.
- **h** We hid ______________ the bushes.

2 Make sentences using the following phrases:

above the clouds	through the supermarket	along the road
during the night	towards the runway	with her friends

Note carefully and remember the prepositions used in these phrases:

divide between (two)	wait for (a person, a thing)
divide among (many)	walk into (a room)
agree with (someone)	part with (something)
agree to (something)	tired of (something)
complain of	different from (something)
ashamed of	full of
angry with	filled with

3 Now make sentences using the phrases in the above list.

4 Select from **a** a suitable adverb to go with each verb in **b** and write a sentence using the two words. Example: The children slept soundly throughout the night.

- **a** painfully stealthily frantically soundly blindly steadily
- **b** marched toiled shouted stampeded crept slept

In **15** we learned how to punctuate a sentence in which a phrase like said Julie or said the policeman broke into the actual words spoken. In those examples we placed a comma after the speaker's name. In the following example, however, note that a full stop has been placed after the speaker's name, because the phrase said the booking-clerk is this time separating two complete sentences and not just parts of one sentence.

"You'll have to hurry," said the booking-clerk. "The train is just going."

5 Punctuate the following sentences:

- **a** We can go no further said the guide our water bottles are empty
- **b** keep still whispered one of the boys they are coming this way
- **c** i have read my book said emma may I have another
- **d** give me a bigger spanner said the mechanic this one is too small
- **e** fasten your seat-belts said the stewardess we are about to land

6 Before punctuating the following sentences, decide whether the examples contain one or two sentences:

- **a** put on your coat said lucys mother before you go out
- **b** we are going home said the boys its time for tea
- **c** dont touch it said philip it might be dangerous
- **d** fetch some coal said my mother and put it on the fire
- **e** what was that exclaimed susan did you hear footsteps

7 Fill the space with the correct form of the adjective in brackets:

- **a** That diamond is the ______________ of all the jewels. (precious)
- **b** Italy is a ______________ country than Britain. (warm)
- **c** Of all the girls Maureen was the ______________. (pretty)
- **d** Yours was the ______________ gift of all. (generous)
- **e** Christopher is the ______________ of the two brothers. (clever)

8 Correct these sentences:

- **a** My sister Sheila is older than me.
- **b** Neither the driver nor the guard were hurt.
- **c** She sang good at the concert last night.
- **d** Laura and me was chosen to act in the school play.
- **e** He didn't give me none of his sweets.
- **f** We didn't see nothing.

21

Read the following description:

> He was a tall, jovial fellow with bushy eyebrows and a pair of very blue eyes which twinkled mischievously when he spoke. His shirt sleeves, rolled above the elbow, revealed powerful arms tanned by sun and wind. His clothes and boots were those of a countryman accustomed to being out of doors in all kinds of weather. It was clear from his build that he was as strong as an ox. He moved slowly and deliberately along the edge of the field, leaving behind him a golden trail of cut grain.

Note the following points:

a The use of adjectives to describe the man's appearance;
b the use of adverbs to give a clear picture of his actions;
c the use of a simile to indicate his strength.

1 Choose one of the three pictures at the top of page 63, and write a description of the person in it. Try to use adjectives, adverbs, and a simile in your description.

2 Write a story about something amusing happening to you at any <u>one</u> of the following places:

a the seaside
b the zoo
c your garden
d the country
e the playing field
f a party
g the street
h the docks

3 Improve these sentences by altering the order of certain words:

a The boy was warned who was making a noise.
b The weather cleared up which had been dull and wet.

c The people were waiting for the bus whom we had seen on the beach.
d The train was leaving the platform which we should have caught.
e The doctor is to be knighted whose discovery saved countless lives.

The man entered the room. He called out in surprise.

These two sentences can be joined in the following way:

a by changing the verb in the first sentence into an ing word, and
b by transferring the words the man to the second sentence to take the place of the pronoun he.

Entering the room, the man called out in surprise.

(Note the comma which takes the place of the full stop.)

The word entering, made by adding ing to the verb enter, is called the present participle of the verb. Remember when forming the present participle of verbs ending with the letter e that these verbs drop the e before adding ing, for example: take – taking, hope – hoping.

4 Join these sentences by changing the verb in the first sentence into a present participle and making any other necessary changes:

a The woman smiled with pleasure. She invited us into her home.
b The men grasped the rope. They pulled with all their might.
c The king rose to his feet. He addressed his subjects.
d The pupil sat down at the desk. She began to write quickly.
e The people talked quietly. They waited for the concert to begin.

These two sentences have been joined by making the verb in the second sentence a present participle and leaving out the pronoun:

The choir boys walked through the snow. They sang Christmas carols.
The choir boys walked through the snow, singing Christmas carols.

5 Join these sentences by the same method:

a The snow fell gently. It covered the landscape with a mantle of white.
b The old man sat at the fire. He nodded sleepily from time to time.
c We heard the bell in the distance. It called the people to worship.
d The girl walked along the street. She gazed happily at the shops.

6 Place the words in each list in order, beginning with the smallest:

a kilogramme, gramme, tonne
b candle, lamp, match, searchlight
c path, road, highway, track, lane
d month, decade, century, day, year

22

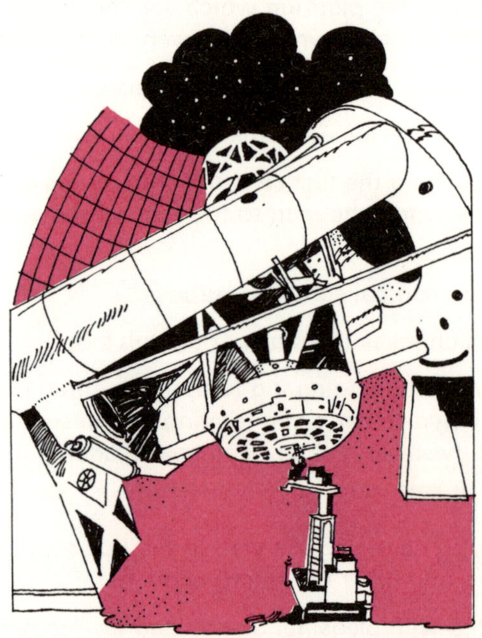

Read this passage carefully:

The Earth upon which we live is one of the known planets that circle the Sun. In ancient times the men who studied the stars noticed that while certain heavenly bodies seemed fixed in the sky, others seemed to move about. The latter they named planets (wanderers). Modern astronomers tell us that the four planets Jupiter, Saturn, Uranus, and Neptune, which are much bigger than the others, are surrounded by poisonous gases and are so cold that any living thing attempting to land on them would immediately be frozen to death. Of the five remaining planets, Venus most closely resembles the Earth in size, but it is a world devoid of moisture, swept unceasingly by storms, and lacking in its atmosphere the life-giving oxygen by which all life is made possible on its nearest neighbour in space – the Earth. Mars is the only planet on which there is any visible sign of life. Most of Mars is desert but there are green areas on its surface which change with the seasons, suggesting that some form of plant life is possible. Little is known of Pluto, the planet furthest from the Sun, but it is known that the surface temperature of one side of Mercury, the hottest and the nearest planet to the Sun, is sufficient to melt lead.

1 Now answer these questions:

a What word means men who study the stars?
b How does a planet differ from a star?

c How many planets are known to circle the Sun?
d Which planet has the highest temperature?
e Give one way in which the planet Venus resembles the Earth.
f What are the green areas on the planet Mars thought to be?
g What two things would make it difficult for anyone attempting to land on Saturn?
h What word in the passage means continually?
i What phrase indicates that there is no water on Venus?
j What two words in the first five lines mean the opposite of each other?
k Write down one thing you have learned about the planet Pluto.
l What would human beings need to have in the atmosphere of a planet in order to live?

2 Replace the underlined phrase by a single word without altering the meaning:

a The waiter brought the list of foods being served.
b The vessel carried many people going off to live in a new land.
c In the cave lived a person who had shut himself off from other people.
d The drought was followed by a great shortage of food.
e Everyone knew of the long and bitter quarrel between the two brothers.
f People who are walking must take care when crossing busy streets.

3 Replace the underlined adverbs by ones of opposite meaning:

a The motorist drove carelessly.
b The queue waited patiently.
c Trains often stop at this station.
d The chieftain advanced proudly.
e Early one morning we struck camp.
f He did the job well.
g The boy spoke politely to her.
h The books lay tidily on the shelf.
i Rapidly the plane gained height.
j The hunter walked recklessly on.

4 Give one word for:

a a practice trial of a play
b something to bring good luck
c the long hair on a lion's neck
d the study of plants and flowers
e love of one's country
f the supplying of water to dry land
g soldiers who fight on foot
h an abandoned and drifting ship
i a crowning ceremony
j a sale at which people bid

5 Form adjectives from these verbs, for example, imagine – imaginary:

forget stick move attract notice attend

Form nouns from these verbs, for example, destroy – destruction:

depart grow advise speak explode serve

23

Read the following sentence carefully, noting the underlined words:

I wrote a letter to Pam, and Sharon has written one too.

The word wrote is the past tense of the verb to write, and the word written is the past participle. The present tense, the past tense, and the past participle are called the principal parts of a verb. Note how the verbs below form their past tense and past participle.

present	**past**	**past participle**
jump	jumped	jumped
catch	caught	caught
write	wrote	written
ring	rang	rung
grow	grew	grown

1 Make a table like the one above and write the principal parts of:

walk	fight	sing	strike	go	choose
sweep	hold	see	bring	break	take

2 Say which word in each bracket is correct:

a Steven has ____________ a hole in his sock. (wore, worn)
b Pete has ____________ the ball over the wall. (threw, thrown)
c Have you ____________ to your father? (spoke, spoken)
d Show me your picture when you have ____________ it. (drew, drawn)
e If I had ____________, I would have told you. (knew, known)
f He has ____________ to bring his pencil. (forgot, forgotten)

In Book 3 you learned some of the following pronouns. These are called personal pronouns because they generally refer to persons.

I he she it we you they mine his hers ours
yours theirs me him her it us you them

The forms my, her, its, our, your, and their are always followed by nouns and are called possessive adjectives.

The following pronouns are called relative pronouns. They are so called because they refer to some noun or pronoun already used in the sentence.

who whose whom which that

3 Find the pronouns in the following sentences, and say whether each is a personal or a relative pronoun:

a Bob returned the book which he had borrowed from me.
b We saw the footballer whose photograph was in the newspaper.
c She spoke of the people she had met on holiday.

- **d** Emma showed him the prize that she had won.
- **e** They found maps which led them to the secret passage.
- **f** The boy who has the new bicycle lives next door to us.

4 In each of the above sentences give the word to which the relative pronoun refers.

An exclamation mark (!) is used after words or phrases spoken or exclaimed by a person who is excited by some feeling or emotion.

Oh! Help! Hurray! Oh dear! How terrible!
What a lovely picture! You careless boy!

Note that an exclamation, even if a single word, begins with a capital letter and ends with an exclamation mark.

"Help!" shouted the drowning man.
"Breakers ahead!" yelled the look-out.

5 Punctuate the following:

- **a** hurray shouted the crowd
- **b** alas sighed the walrus
- **c** oh dear cried the girl in dismay
- **d** what a terrible sight gasped the old lady
- **e** you miserable wretch said the king to the thieving servant

6 Correct the following sentences:

- **a** Tell Andrew and I what you seen when you was there.
- **b** Sally is a better swimmer than me.
- **c** The money was divided among Bob and I.
- **d** Neither the letter nor the parcel have been posted.
- **e** In the corner was his bat and ball.
- **f** "Can I go to the pictures tonight?" asked Yvonne.
- **g** Me and him went hiking last summer.
- **h** I won't never do that again.
- **i** He said that he hasn't got none.

7 Choose one of the following subjects and give a talk on it to the class:

- **a** space travel
- **b** Arctic animals
- **c** famous explorers
- **d** keeping pets
- **e** road safety
- **f** a memorable visit

24

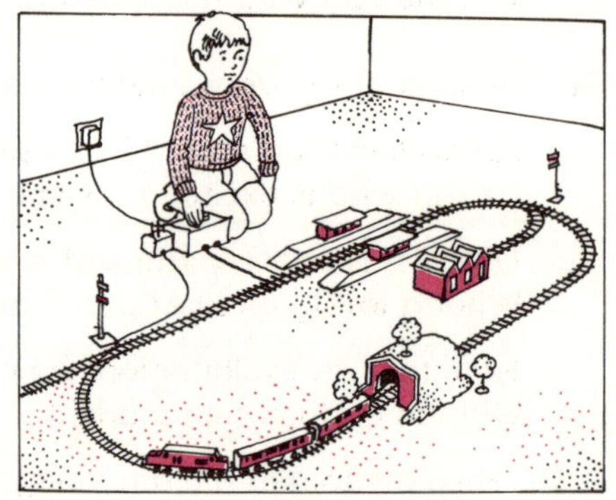

1 The boy in the picture is obviously enjoying himself very much. He is controlling a model railway system which he has assembled. In order to find out how he did this, turn to page 63. Study the pictures on the bottom half of the page and then describe the various stages in the building of a model railway.

2 Describe clearly how you would do any one of the following:

- **a** make tea
- **b** phone for an ambulance
- **c** sew on a button
- **d** make a kite
- **e** rescue a person from drowning
- **f** mend a puncture
- **g** read a map
- **h** fish for minnows

3 This letter was sent to Vicky Hughes by her friend Linda Ashton:

14, Westburn Avenue
Dalton
6th March 1976

Dear Vicky,

I am sorry to say that my ten-year old brother, Sam, is ill. I am doing my best to entertain him, but I need your help. Do you know of any good game I could play with him? He has to remain in bed for some days. Your brother Tim might be able to suggest some good game too.

Yours sincerely,
Linda.

Imagine that you are Vicky or Tim. Write a reply to that letter.

4 Write a postcard asking for a catalogue of sports goods which was advertised by Messrs Dickson and Lambe whose shop is at 121 Ford Street, Harlington. The paper in which you saw the advertisement was the *Daily Citizen*. How would you complete both sides of the postcard?

Note carefully how the following sentences are joined:

a That lady is our teacher. You spoke to her.
That lady to whom you spoke is our teacher.

b The box was damaged. The goods arrived in it.
The box in which the goods arrived was damaged.

5 Join the following sentences by using which or whom in place of the underlined pronouns:

a The reporter asked for the name of the girl. The first prize had been awarded to her.
b This is a map of the island. We lived on it for two years.
c Our friends are coming to visit us. We stayed with them at Easter.
d The train was fast and comfortable. We travelled on it.
e The transmitter was damaged by the storm. We receive our television programmes from it.
f Sally Briggs has left the district. I was very friendly with her.
g The country is famous for its wines. I have just come from it.
h The farmer has over a hundred hens. My mother buys eggs from him.
i The school concert was a great success. We took part in it.
j The mountains were wild and rugged. The plane flew over them.

Brian Shaw has arranged to go to the cinema tonight with a friend who is coming from some distance away. His friend travelling in the direction of the arrow, is arriving by bus at the stop marked A. The cinema is marked B on the map. Give a clear account of the instructions which Brian would have to give his friend to ensure that he arrived at the cinema where they were both to meet.

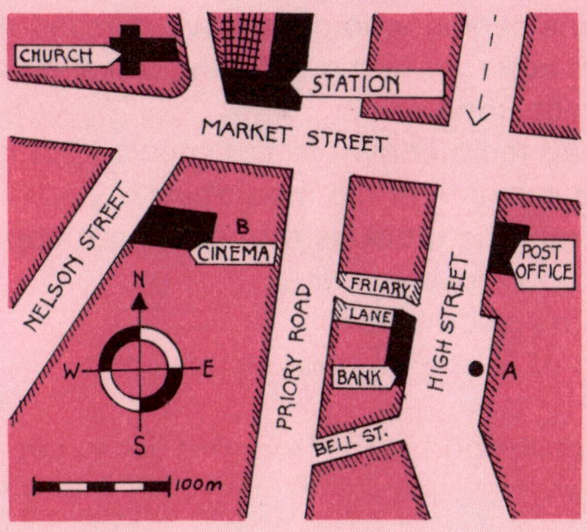

25

Read this passage carefully:

Never shall I forget the sight of those three towering peaks in the early sunlight of the following morning. High above us, up into the blue air, soared their twisted snow-wreaths. Beneath the snow-line the peaks were purple with heaths, and so were the wild moors that ran up the slopes towards them. Straight before us the white ribbon of Solomon's Great Road stretched away uphill to the foot of the centre peak, about five miles away, and there stopped. At last we were drawing near to the wonderful mines that had been the cause of the miserable death of the old Portuguese Dom three centuries ago, of his ill-starred descendant, and also, as we feared, of George Curtis, Sir Henry's brother. On we went, till we saw before us, and between ourselves and the peak, a vast circular hole with sloping sides, three hundred or more feet in depth, and over half a mile round.

"Can't you guess what that is?" I said to Sir Henry and Good, who were staring at the awful pit before us. They shook their heads.

"Then it is clear that you have never seen the diamond diggings at Kimberley. You may depend on it that this is Solomon's Diamond Mine."

At the edge of this vast hole, which was the pit marked on the old Dom's map, the Great Road branched into two and circumvented it.

(from *King Solomon's Mines* by H. Rider Haggard)

1 Begin your answer to each question with the underlined words:

- **a** Where did Solomon's Great Road stop?
- **b** What kind of country lay between them and the peaks?
- **c** What do you think they had come in search of?
- **d** How many people had previously come this way on the same quest?
- **e** Of those, name one person who must have reached the pit.
- **f** How old was the map that had guided the travellers to where they stood?
- **g** Where did the Great Road end?
- **h** What place seemed to be known to the speaker but not to his friends?
- **i** What covered the summits of the mountains?
- **j** Write the words from the brackets that could not apply to the Great Road. (level, purple, straight, snow-covered)
- **k** What was Sir Henry's surname?
- **l** Give the meaning of ill-starred and circumvented.

2 Choose suitable adjectives and verbs from this list to complete each of the sentences on the opposite page:

watchful reeled lame withered pounced drooped appetizing
simmered limped mountainous stricken unsuspecting

a The ______ dog ______ down the street.
b An ______ stew ______ on the stove.
c The ______ cat ______ on the ______ mouse.
d The ______ flowers ______ in the vase.
e The ______ ship ______ under the blows of the ______ seas.

3 Each of the trawler skippers mentioned in the table below returned from the fishing grounds with the biggest catch for his particular port over a given period. Study the table and then answer the questions below.

Port	Trawler	Skipper	Total catch (kits)	Area fished	Date landed	Length of trip (days)
HULL	Kingston Emerald	S. Duffield	3,601	Bear Island	Jan. 4	21
GRIMSBY	Royal Lincs	J. Ferrand	3,312	White Sea	Dec. 28	24
LOWESTOFT	Boston Hunter	I. Prior	150	North Sea	Jan. 11	13
MILFORD	Almadine	A. Harvey	339	Porcupine Bank	Jan. 17	14
FLEETWOOD	Carella	S. Christie	1,450	White Sea	Jan. 2	27
ABERDEEN	Ben Lui	H. Bowman	702	Faroe	Jan. 5	15

(*By permission of the editor of "World Fishing"*)

a Name the skipper who landed the biggest catch.
b At what port was the next biggest catch landed?
c Which trawler spent exactly a fortnight at sea?
d In what sea did the *Boston Hunter* fish?
e Which trawler arrived home before New Year's Day?
f To which port did Skipper Bowman return?
g Of the two trawlers fishing in the White Sea, which spent most days at sea?
h Write the surnames of the skippers in alphabetical order.

26

Certain words are written sometimes with a capital and sometimes with a small letter. study the following examples, paying particular attention to the underlined words. In group A these words are printed with capital letters and in group B with small letters.

	A	B
a	We met Father and Mother.	Their fathers and mothers came.
b	I visited Uncle Bob.	This boy has three uncles.
c	We saw Doctor Harris.	They asked us to call a doctor.
d	In walked Captain Starke.	The ship was without a captain.
e	The enemy feared Admiral Hawke.	The story was about a famous admiral.
f	They cheered Queen Elizabeth.	I like to read about kings and queens.
g	He was the son of Earl Storr.	The estate was owned by an earl.

1 Write the following sentences, putting in the necessary capitals:

a we received a postcard from aunt sarah and uncle george.
b a message was quickly sent to doctor jones.
c in history books we read about many famous admirals and generals.
d queen elizabeth, accompanied by prince philip, attended the ball.
e sharon went out with mother but I stayed at home with father.
f a ship's captain has a job of great responsibility.

Inverted commas are used to denote actual words spoken. If the name of the person spoken to is used, that name is separated by a comma (or commas) from the rest of the sentence.

"Bring your exercise to me, John, when you have finished it."
"Sally, please fetch some fresh water for the flowers."
"Your work in geography is improving, Tom."

2 Write the following sentences with correct punctuation:

a i am sorry captain starke that i was not at the docks to meet you this afternoon
b this is my daughter sir of whom you have heard me speak
c vicky tell mummy that uncle tom and aunt betty have arrived

The pronouns who, whose, whom, which, and what are sometimes used to begin sentences that ask questions. When they are so used, they are called interrogative pronouns.

Who can answer my question?
Which did you choose?
Whom did you see?
What are you doing?
Whose coat is this?

3 Write five sentences using each of the above interrogative pronouns.

4 In the following sentences change all singulars into plurals:

- **a** The child watched the workman putting a slate on the roof of the house.
- **b** The housewife cut the potato with a sharp knife.
- **c** The donkey and the ox chased the goose and the sheep.
- **d** The trout was packed in a box and sent to the city.

The two verbs learn and teach are often incorrectly used:

to learn means to gain knowledge or skill
to teach means to give a lesson or to instruct

5 Use the correct form of learn or teach to complete these sentences:

- **a** Miss Brown ____________ us history and geography.
- **b** I would like to ____________ French.
- **c** Jimmy Travers promised to ____________ me how to swim.
- **d** I hope that I shall ____________ quickly.
- **e** If I ____________ quickly, I'll be able to ____________ my little brother when we go to the seaside.

6 Correct the following sentences:

- **a** My sister and me have saved our pocket-money.
- **b** Mum, can I stay up to watch the film tonight?
- **c** Who did you give the money to?
- **d** We will be on holiday in a few weeks' time.
- **e** She is much bigger than me.
- **f** Where did you say you seen it?
- **g** The old man walked very slow.
- **h** Each of the children were given a book.
- **i** Neither of these comics belong to me.

27

1 In joining the following sentences, decide whether to use (1) who, which, whom, whose <u>or</u> (2) a participle ending in <u>ing</u>:

- **a** There is the newspaper. We read the report of the discovery in it.
- **b** The man has gone abroad. My father bought this house from him.
- **c** The girl has gone to the dentist. Her tooth was aching.
- **d** The boy clung to the ledge. He shouted for help.
- **e** The man was arrested. He had stolen the money.

2 Choose suitable verbs, adverbs, and adjectives from this list to complete each of the sentences below:

violently	heavy	staggered	gently	lurched
exhausted	swerved	meandered	lurked	dim

- **a** The car ____________ ____________ to avoid the child.
- **b** A ____________ figure ____________ in the shadows.
- **c** The ____________ mountaineer ____________ to the summit.
- **d** The little stream ____________ ____________ through the wood.
- **e** The vessel ____________ in the ____________ seas.

3 Re-write the following sentences, choosing in each case the correct word from the brackets:

The (bow, bough) of the (beach, beech) tree was (to, too, two) (weak, week) to (bare, bear) the (wait, weight) of the (boy, buoy).

4 Write the sentences given below, replacing the underlined words with phrases taken from this list:

high and dry	might and main	high and low
hue and cry	spick and span	safe and sound

- **a** We searched <u>everywhere</u>
- **b** The wrestler strove with <u>all his power</u>.
- **c** Everything in the room was <u>tidy</u>.
- **d** The child was found <u>uninjured</u>.
- **e** The <u>noise of pursuit</u> was heard.
- **f** The boat was left <u>out of the water</u>.

5 Punctuate the following:

- **a** im going on holiday said valerie to the kennel-maid could you please look after my puppy for me until 24th of august
- **b** help shouted brenda ive been stung by a wasp

6 Compare these adjectives:

proud good red dry tough

7 Explain in a sentence what the job of each person is. (Example – An actor is a man who plays on the stage or in films.):

actor	composer	surveyor	solicitor
sculptor	milliner	stationer	tailor

8 Draw this table and complete it:

present	past	past participle
go	______	______
______	______	seen
______	ate	______
______	______	done
______	wrote	______

9 Write these sentences, choosing in each case the correct word from the brackets:

- **a** The reward was divided (between, among) the two boys.
- **b** Tom's mother was very proud (of, off) his success.
- **c** Bob at last agreed (with, to) Steve's plan.
- **d** We waited (for, on) our friends at the bus-stop.
- **e** This is different (from, than) that.

10 Change the nouns in the following sentences from masculine to feminine gender, altering other words where necessary:

- **a** The landlord sent for his son and his nephew.
- **b** The prince remained a bachelor all his life.
- **c** The mayor was at the station to welcome the marquis.
- **d** The boy went to the circus with his father and brother.

11 Divide this sentence into subject and predicate and then answer the questions below:

The old gardener was planting potatoes at the bottom of his large garden.

- **a** What is the verb in the above sentence?
- **b** What is the gender of the noun gardener?
- **c** Give two prepositions from the sentence.
- **d** Write the singular of the noun potatoes.
- **e** Give an adjective from the sentence.

28

Read this passage carefully:

Sarah's one delight in life was to be hugged, and to hug in return. If I held her to my chest and supported her with one arm, I found that she clung with less painful tenacity; but her favourite perch was always across my shoulders, and no matter where she started off, she slowly crept upwards, a few inches at a time, hoping that I would not notice, until she was lying across my shoulders. At first she could not bear to be put on the ground and would bellow forlornly. When you picked her up, you could feel her heart beating like a trip hammer, and she would clutch you frantically. She did not object to being on the ground providing she could hang on to some part of you, even your foot, for it gave her a feeling of security.

When she was about a month old, she grew less scared of being on the ground, but she liked to feel that Jacquie or I was near. Her sight, like that of all ant-eaters, was very bad and if you moved more than five feet away from her, she could not see you, even if you moved.

(From *The Drunken Forest* by Gerald Durrell)

- **a** What kind of animal was Sarah?
- **b** What was her favourite perch?
- **c** What happened if she was put on the ground?
- **d** What gave her a feeling of security?
- **e** How old was she when she became less afraid of being on the ground?
- **f** Could Sarah see well?
- **g** Write the meaning of: tenacity, forlornly, frantically.
- **h** What is a trip hammer?

The Children of the New Forest, written by Captain Marryat, tells what happened to the four children of Colonel Beverley, a Cavalier officer who lost his life at the battle of Naseby in the service of King Charles I. Oliver Cromwell and his soldiers had rebelled against the King. After the defeat and capture of the King, some of Cromwell's soldiers sought out and plundered the houses of those who had fought on the King's side. Arnwood, the home of Colonel Beverley, was near the New Forest. The Colonel's wife, heart-broken at the death of her husband, had died soon after, leaving the children in the care of an elderly relative. In addition, the children had a trusted friend in an old and faithful forester named Jacob Armitage who had promised his master that whatever happened he would protect the children. Jacob lived in a cottage in the New Forest, not far from Arnwood. One day, while hunting, he heard the sound of horses. Now look at the pictures and answer the questions.

a Who are the soldiers in the first picture?
b Why is Jacob Armitage taking great care to avoid being seen?
c Whose house is shown in the second picture?
d Where do you think the children are going? Who warned them to leave?
e What are the forester and the boy watching?
f At the cottage everyone had certain jobs to do. Describe the jobs you see being done.

29

(See lesson 5)

(See lesson 10)

(See lesson 21)

(See lesson 24)

30

These short messages all say the same thing. Can you work them out?

a hist si het astl agep fo het astl ookb fo het eriess. hatw artp idd ouy ikel estb

b 2.7.1948 5.36 p.m.

thex thisx lastx pagex thex bookx isx ofx lastx
seriesx ofx likex partx youx bestx thex didx whatx

c

In **a** the first letter of each word has been moved to the end of the word.

b is a date code. The numbers tell you which order the words should be written in to make sense. The second word in line one should be written first, then the seventh word in line one. When you have solved line one, you do exactly the same thing with line two. This code never has more than nine words in a line. You ignore the xs.

c is based on this diagram:

A	B	C
D	E	F
G	H	I

J	K	L
M	N	O
P	Q	R

S	T	U
V	W	X
Y	Z	

A is written as ┘, H is written as ⊓ N is written as ⊡, R is written as ┌·, W is written as ⊡, V is written as ⊐.

All these coded passages are taken from passages in this book. Can you decode them and discover which passage they come from? The codes used are the ones used for the messages above.

a utb het inimentl snti oisonousp tsi eantm ot eb akent nternallyi lthougha otn ni akesc ontw ouy ellt rsm llana os arillam

b 4.6.1985 2.37p.m.
usx ofx solomonsx straightx ribbonx beforex greatx whitex thex
awayx footx ofx roadx thex stretchedx thex tox uphillx
aboutx andx therex centrex awayx stoppedx milesx fivex.

c

Now use one of these codes to write a message of your own. Can your friend solve it?